An Essential Manual of the Anthropologist's Fieldwork in Peru

Ricardo L Sabogal

An Essential Manual of the Anthropologist's Fieldwork in Peru

Ricardo L Sabogal

Sociedad Peruana de Antropología Visual

Universidad Nacional de Trujillo-CEPRODE

Universidad Nacional de San Antonio Abad del Cusco

About the author

Ricardo L Sabogal is Peruvian anthropologist and founding member of "Sociedad Peruana de Antropología Visual". Sabogal has done fieldwork in Verona and Perugia in Italy; Tambomachay, the Amazonia, and Huanchaco in Perú; Texas, New York, New Jersey, Philadelphia, Delaware, and Florida in the United States of America.

Books of the author are Lagartos' Club; The No Theory of the Citizens; Proactivity and

Reactivity in the Andes and Amazonia; Paleoaxiology: The Resurrection of Dormant Values; Egoculture: Anthropology of the Individual; Forgiving the Gods; Tup the Fisher; Live and Die in Tambomachay; The Spanish Teacher; The Romantic Latin Piano Guitar Man; The Insurrectionist Anthropologist; Magnanimous; The Wrong Tourist; The Peruvians; History's Original Natural Born Surfers; A Primitive Anthropologist in the USA; The Illegal Anthropologist; and Privileged People without Pockets.

Dedicated to the memory of
Moisés Sabogal Urbina, Mamá
Balbina, Papá Roberto, José
María Arguedas, and Salatiel
Romero Malca.

To Jeanine, my family, my friends, and my colleagues.

Contents

Preface and Acknowledgements

Interculturalism, new worldviews, multiculturalism, cultural conflicts, better diffusion of ideas, social media, faster communications, migration, and so on are our omnipresent reality. Although these phenomena are no new, they are increasing at alarming rate. We know anthropology is the science-art that deals with those human facts, and consequently anthropologists have the professional responsibility to study all these events of our global culture. I truly think this is the perfect moment for the success of modern anthropologists.

Fieldwork is the most difficult task in the professional life of an anthropologist, and it is the most important mission for any research. A wrong simple question can cause bias and ignorance, and a minute prejudice can cause a big mistake. Nobody can teach you how to do a proper fieldwork, and nobody without experience in the fieldwork can tell you anything about fieldwork. Expert fieldworkers can just give you advices about fieldwork, and after that, you will be alone in the field. Maybe these advices seem obvious, easy, or bizarre, but believe me, if you don't review them everyday, then you will forget them while doing your interviews, observations or whatever you do in the field.

Traditional fieldwork, traditional anthropology, and traditional ethnography are very dangerous. Concepts and entities like indigenous people, ethnic group, indians, cultures, race, multiculturalism, cultural relativism, nonprofit organizations, academicism, and so on, feed our most terrible injustices.

I hope that this small book is helpful to change many wrong ideas.

Let me take this opportunity to thank the numerous first-class colleagues and excellent professors of mine who have helped me to become an anthropologist. Thanks to José Becerra Castañeda, Aurelio Carmona, Washington Rozas, Jorge Flores Ochoa, Eduardo Achútegui, Orlando Velásquez, José Escalante, José Elias Minaya, José Coronado, Mario Morvelí, Marco Villasante, Ricardo Valderrama, José Gonzales Rios, Gabriel Escobar, Mario Millones, Ramiro Ccoscco, Hugo Blanco, Carlos Quispe, David Mottocanchi, Julio César Farfán, Liliana Mercado, Selena Cervantes, Erik Fuentes, Herman

Pancorbo, Rosa Paredes, Efraín Candia, Carmen Olivera, Edwin Rodriguez, Maquela Rozas, Alex Alvarez, Carmen Rosa Araoz, Roberto Quispe, Daniel, Víctor, Marcial, Yoni, Valentín, José, Don Bernardino, Fabiana, Rosa Huaracha, Shirley Luna, Gervasio Achircana, Edgard Pelaez Vinces, and many other good anthropologists.

Thank you very much, and

God bless you all,

Ricardo L Sabogal

6

José María Arguedas
Finest Peruvian anthropologist. You must
read his books.

8

Basics

We can find a lot of excellent books about fieldworks, methods, ethnographies, fieldnotes, research designs, writing, editing, publishing, techniques, interviewing, observations, qualitative inquiry, focus groups, qualitative methods, quantitative methods, qualitative data analysis, quantitative data analysis, coding manuals, case studies, evaluation methods, grounded methods, etcetera, etcetera, etcetera. We need them because we are anthropologists of course, but the

MOST WE NEED IS TO LEARN THE BASICS OF ANTHROPOLOGY. THE FIELDWORK IS LIKE A BUILDING: STRONG BASE, THEN STRONG FIELDWORK.

STUDENTS HATE EXTENSIVE BOOKS. THEY SAY THAT WE ANTHROPOLOGISTS CAN COMMUNICATE THE SAME THINGS IN LESS PAGES AND CHAPTERS, AND I THINK THEY ARE RIGHT, SO LET'S SEE THE BASICS ONLY.

PRINCIPLES: YOU MUST OWN MORAL BELIEFS AND RULES. YOU ARE NOT A MACHINE, YOU ARE NOT A MICROSCOPE, AND YOU ARE NOT A MERCENARY. REMEMBER THIS ALL THE TIME. IF YOU DON'T HAVE

PRINCIPLES, YOU SHOULD NOT DO ANTHROPOLOGY IN PERU. WITHOUT PRINCIPLES MAYBE YOU WILL BE IN PERU DOING SOMETHING AS A MINING COMPANY MERCENARY OR SOMETHING ELSE.

SPANISH: No SPANISH, NO COMMUNICATION, AND NO COMMUNICATION, NO ANTHROPOLOGY. TRANSLATORS ARE BAD IDEA, AND IN FACT, THE BEST ANTHROPOLOGIST FOR DOING RESEARCH IN PERU IS A PERUVIAN ANTHROPOLOGIST, THERE ARE THOUSANDS OF EXCELLENT PERUVIAN ANTHROPOLOGISTS, BUT THE PROBLEM IS THAT

OLIGARCHIC MONEY IS FOR OLIGARCHIC ANTHROPOLOGISTS.

MOTIVATION: WHY ARE YOU GOING TO PERU? MONEY? SCHOLARSHIP? MASTERS DEGREE? PhD DEGREE? VACATIONS? BOYFRIEND? GIRLFRIEND? PARENTS? YOU REALLY NEED A STRONG MOTIVATION. THE BEST ANTHROPOLOGISTS I KNEW WERE PASSIONATE AND THEY WANTED JUSTICE FOR VICTIMS. THEY WERE IDEALISTS, WEIRD, AND EXTREMELY ENTHUSIASTIC.

ANTHROPOLOGY: YOU NEED THE BASICS OF ANTHROPOLOGY! THEORIES,

CONCEPTS, METHODS, TECHNIQUES, AND HISTORY. YOU DON'T NEED TO BE AN EXPERT, JUST THE BASICS. ANTHROPOLOGISTS WHO KNOW ABOUT THE CONCEPT OF CULTURE AND OTHER BASIC CONCEPTS ARE IN BETTER SHAPE THAN ANTHROPOLOGISTS WHO KNOW A LOT ABOUT MANY SOPHISTICATED THEORIES BUT KNOW NOTHING ABOUT BASIC IDEAS.

ANTHROPOLOGISTS:

YOU MUST KNOW ABOUT PERUVIAN ANTHROPOLOGISTS AND THEIR WORKS. IF YOU WANT TO KNOW SOMETHING GENERAL ABOUT PERU, YOU HAVE TO READ PERUVIAN AUTHORS, NO EUROPEAN, ASIAN OR NORTH AMERICAN AUTHORS. WHY?

BECAUSE THERE IS A HUGE DIFFERENCE BETWEEN PERUVIAN AND ALIEN, AND BECAUSE THERE IS A HUGE DIFFERENCE BETWEEN 'TOUCH-AND-GO' BOOKS AND LIFETIME'S WORKS.

BASIC PERUVIAN BOOKS FOR ANTHROPOLOGISTS ARE:

EL PENSAMIENTO MÁGICO RELIGIOSO EN EL PERÚ CONTEMPORÁNEO, LA IDIOSINCRASIA DE OCCIDENTE, HISTORIA DE NUESTRO TIEMPO, AND DESARROLLO POLÍTICO DE LA CIVILIZACIÓN ANDINA OF FERNANDO SILVA SANTISTEBAN.

HORAS DE LUCHA, AND PáGINAS LIBRES OF MANUEL GONZáLEZ PRADA.

EL MUNDO ES ANCHO Y AJENO, LA SERPIENTE DE ORO, AND LOS PERROS HAMBRIENTOS OF CIRO ALEGRíA.

LOS RíOS PROFUNDOS, TODAS LAS SANGRES, YAWAR FIESTA, EL ZORRO DE ARRIBA Y EL ZORRO DE ABAJO, EL SEXTO, LA AGONíA DE RASU ÑITI, DIOSES Y HOMBRES DE HUAROCHIRí, CANTO KECHWA, AND MITOS, LEYENDAS Y CUENTOS PERUANOS OF JOSé MARíA ARGUEDAS.

ESTRUCTURAS ANDINAS DEL PODER OF
MARÍA ROSTWOROWSKI.

LOS GALLINAZOS SIN PLUMAS OF JULIO
RAMÓN RIBEYRO.

DESBORDE POPULAR Y CRISIS DEL
ESTADO OF JOSÉ MATOS MAR.

SIETE ENSAYOS DE INTERPRETACIÓN
DE LA REALIDAD PERUANA OF JOSÉ CARLOS
MARIÁTEGUI.

EL TUNGSTENO AND PACO YUNQUE OF
CÉSAR VALLEJO.

REDOBLE POR RANCAS OF MANUEL SCORZA.

GREGORIO CONDORI MAMANI OF RICARDO VALDERRAMA.

AMAZONIA 500 AÑOS OF OSCAR PAREDES PANDO.

PASTORES DE PARATÍA OF JORGE FLORES OCHOA.

JUECES ANDINOS OF JOSÉ CANAL.

Al borde del naufragio of Rodrigo Montoya.

VISA: You have to go to the Peruvian Embassy for your visa. Many anthropologists go to Peru with no visa because they just need their passports. Peruvians need visa to enter in a North American country or European country and they pay a lot of money for a visa at any embassy. If Peruvians work overseas without a proper visa, then they are illegals, consequently if you go to Peru without a proper visa

THEN YOU WILL BE AN ILLEGAL TOO. UNFORTUNATELY, MANY ALIEN ANTHROPOLOGISTS AND ARCHEOLOGISTS GO TO PERU WITH TOURIST VISAS ONLY, AND THEY EVEN WORK WITHOUT AUTHORIZATION FOR MINING COMPANIES AND OTHERS PRIVATE INTERESTS WHO STEAL LANDS, ARTIFACTS, AND RESOURCES.

<u>SACRIFICE</u>: DOING ANTHROPOLOGY IN PERU IS NOT A VACATION. YOU MUST BE PREPARED TO MAKE SACRIFICES AND ONLY IF YOU REALLY ARE PREPARED, GO TO PERU.

<u>LOCAL PARTNER</u>: YOU NEED LOCAL ANTHROPOLOGISTS OR ARCHEOLOGISTS AS PARTNERS AND COAUTHORS. MANY NAMES WILL BE ON YOUR BOOK OR PAPER, AND OF COURSE, YOU HAVE TO PAY THE LOCAL ANTHROPOLOGISTS AND ARCHEOLOGISTS. WITHOUT LOCAL ANTHROPOLOGISTS OR ARCHEOLOGISTS IS IMPOSSIBLE TO DO RESEARCH IN PERU. IT IS VERY COMMON THAT MANY ALIEN ANTHROPOLOGISTS AND ARCHEOLOGISTS STEAL INFORMATION FROM LOCAL ANTHROPOLOGISTS AND ARCHEOLOGISTS AND THEY DON'T RECOGNIZE THE SOURCES OF INFORMATION. AMAZINGLY, WE CAN SEE

ONLY THE NAMES OF ALIEN ANTHROPOLOGISTS.

Source: Ricardo L Sabogal. Trujillo.

You can find everywhere original and ancient stories.

Why?

Why Peru? Peru is one of the most interesting

countries in the world for an anthropologist

because is unique. Frankly, you can find

whatever you want in Peru. In this amazing

and unique country, you can find 84 of 114

identified living areas in our planet Earth. Peru

is an Amazonian country, a mountainy land,

and a coastal nation. In Peru you can find a

culturally diverse population, more than 50

languages, a variety of religions, unbelievable

stories, very strange societies, strong racism,

present colonialism and slavery,

multiculturalism, interculturalism, spectacular

folklores, catchy traditions, ancient noble

values, singular kinships, just name it.

Surprisingly, we know almost nothing about
Peruvian cultures because abusive invaders
destroyed Peruvian history.

Source: Universidad Nacional de Trujillo.
College students protesting in famous
Huaca de la Luna.

Who

Who can do anthropology in Peru? Only anthropology students? Only professional anthropologists with bachelor, master or PhD degree? No. Everybody can do anthropology in Peru, but remember, if you are going to Peru to steal knowledge or materials, you are not going to do anthropology in Peru because that is not anthropology. This new century is bizarre since mercenary anthropologists, some bad nonprofit organizations and nongovernmental organizations, armies, and greedy mining companies are doing bad anthropology to support rich people. Also there are too much NGOs that pay particular attention to money and forget about people and their needs, and there are too many anthropologists and archeologists who are entitled to do whatever they want in the field.

The best part is that you can choose to become a decent person.

Source: Andrés A. Caballero H. and Gregorio Santos Guerrero. Pulán, Peru. Salatiel Romero Malca was Peruvian anthropologist and mayor of Pulán who defended his people against mining companies.

How

You need a strong reason, enough money, and good Peruvian friends. Your reason is very personal, money is always available through scholarships and the proper channels, and you can find Peruvians friends online or at any Peruvian or South American club. If you search online through universities or anthropology clubs web sites, you will find Peruvians who love anthropology. The reality is that if you really want to go to Peru, then you will go there anyway.

SOURCE: TITO LESCANO.
THE PERUVIAN FLAG.

LANGUAGES

Spanish is mandatory. Translators? Interpreters? No way! You will need a translator if you deal with Quechua, Aymara, or any Amazonian nation or society only. Language is the most important aspect of any culture, so you need to learn Spanish if you want to do a decent research, unfortunately in the majority of cases almost all fieldworks made by no Spanish speaking anthropologists were wrong because cultural and language barriers in the field.

Many Peruvian societies and communities are wrongly

named and some of them are:

Arawac

Ashaninka

Chamicuro

Culina

Machiguenga

Nomatsiguenga

Yine

Cahuapana

Chayahuita

Harakmbut

Huitoto

Bora

Ocaina

Jíbaro

Achual

Aguaruna

Candochi

Huambisa

Pano

Amahuaca

Capanahua

Cashibo-Cacataibo

Cashinahua   Mayuruna-

Matsé

Nahua

Sharanahua

Shipibo-Conibo

Yaminahua

Peba-Yagua

Yagua

Quechua

Quechua del Napo

Quechua del Pastaza y del

Tigre

Quechua Lamista y Kiwcha-
Runa

Tacana

Ese'Ejja

Tucano

Secoya

Tupi-Guarani

Cocama-Cocamilla

Zaparo

Arabela

This list is only a small part
of all languages and

dialects that are present in Peru.

Language is not only words or sounds, language is the whole communication: faces, tones, postures, subliminal intentions, gestures, and so on. Language is the invisible vibe that we can feel if we pay attention.

When we are in Peru we need a basic vocabulary, these words are properly 'Peruvian words' and many of them have different meanings in different contexts. You can find these words in other countries but they are not the same.

TENTATIVE PERUVIAN BASIC VOCABULARY FOR AN ANTHROPOLOGIST

Almost all Spanish words are polysemic and therefore they have many possible meanings.

Agarrar

Verb. Take something or to kiss somebody, depending on the context.

Amigo, Feminine Amiga

Noun. Friend, guy, hey, sir, excuse me, depending on the context.

Apu

Noun. God, sacred mountain.

Arriba Perú

Encouragement. Up Peru!

Asado, feminine asada

Noun, and adjective. Angry, barbecue, roast, depending on the context.

Atorrante

Noun. Idiot, stupid, snob, nasty, depending on the context.

Autoridad

Noun. Person who has power and who gives orders.

Borracho, feminine borracha

Noun. Drunk.

Broder

Noun. Brother, friend, hey, guy, hello, depending on the context.

Brujo, feminine bruja

Noun. Witch doctor, witch, bad person, magician, depending on the context.

Burro, feminine burra

Noun. Donkey, stupid, idiot, depending on the cotext.

Cabecear

Verb. Hit with the head, cheat. Depending on the context.

Cachaco, feminine cachaca

Noun. Soldier.

Calato, feminie calata

Noun. Naked, poor, without money, depending on the context.

Campesino, feminine campesina

Noun. Farmer, peasant, poor people, depending on the context.

Campo

Noun. Countryside, field, space, land, depending on the context.

Canillita

Noun. Poor, child, poor child, poor child worker, depending on the context.

Caramba

Noun, soft word. Damn.

Católico, feminine católica

Noun. Catholic but in a Peruvian way. Virgin Mary is extremely important and Apus and local gods are present too.

Cebichito

Noun. Peruvian meal, raw fish and lime, onions and hot peppers.

Chamán or Paqo

Noun. Witch doctor.

Chamba

Noun. Work or job.

Chape

Noun. Kiss.

Chato, feminine chata

Noun. Small guy.

Chelas

Noun. Beers.

Chino, feminine china.

Noun. Chinese, guy, hello, depending on the context.

Chisme

Noun. Gossip.

Chismoso, feminine chismosa

Noun. Scandalmonger.

Chochera

Noun. Buddy, dude, hey, brother, friend.

Cholo, feminine chola

Noun. Brother, friend, stupid, poor, ignorant, mestizo, depending on the context.

Choro, feminine chora

Noun. Mussel, thief, depending on the context.

Chupar

Verb. Drink alcoholic drinks.

Ciudadano, feminine ciudadana

Noun. Citizen.

Coca

Noun. Coca leaf and is not a drug, and is sacred in some parts of the country.

Comida

Noun. Food.

Compañero, feminine compañera

Noun. Fellow, mate, hey, comrade, partner, depending on the context.

Comparito, feminine comadre

Noun. Hello, hey, brother, buddy, friend, mate.

Compadre, feminine comadre

Noun. Godfather or godmother of one's child, or father or mother of one's godchild.

Comunero, feminine comunera

Noun. Member of a community of campesinos.

Comunidad

Noun. Community, community of campesinos, small town, village, club, depending of the context.

Contactos

Noun. Network, acquaintances, friends, partners, depending of the context.

Crudo, feminine cruda.

Noun. Foreigner, gringo, raw, depending of the context.

Cuaderno

Noun. Notebook.

Cuero

Noun. Cute, beautiful person, pretty woman or man, handsome, leather, depending of the context.

Cuñao or cuñado, feminine cuñada

Noun. Buddy, hey, brother or sister in law, hello, depending of the context.

Doctor, feminine doctora

Noun. Hello, sir, mister, madam, hey, lawyer, doctor, physician, doc, buddy, depending of the context.

Ecología

Noun. Ecology, land, nature, environment, depending of the context.

Encuesta

Noun. Survey.

Entrevista

Noun. Interview.

Estudio

Noun. Research, paper, investigation, book, ethnography, fieldwork, depending of the context.

Etnografía

Noun. Ethnography.

Evaluación

Noun. Evaluation, assessment, depending of the context.

Familia

Noun. Family, relatives, friends, extended family, nuclear family, buddy, depending of the context.

Flaco, feminine flaca

Noun. Hello, buddy, guy, person, hey, depending of the context.

Floro

Noun. Blah, blah, blah.

Fotografía

Noun. Picture.

Gordo, feminine gorda.

Noun. Fat, buddy, depending of the context.

Gringo, feminine gringa.

Noun. Foreigner, blonde, US citizen, depending of the context.

Hacendado, feminine hacendada

Noun. Big farmer.

Hambre

Noun. Hungry.

Hamuy

Verb. Come (Quechua language).

Hembra

Noun. Girl, woman, female, girlfriend, depending of the context.

Hemoliente or emoliente

Noun. Infusion, extract, or remedy.

Huaca

Noun. Sacred place, ruins, archeological site, pyramid, ancient building, depending of the context.

Huachafo, feminine huachafa

Noun. Snob, tacky, stupid, poor, ignorant, pretentious, depending of the context.

Indio, feminine india

Noun. Mestizo, stupid, poor, ignorant, aborigine, nasty, depending of the context.

Informante

Noun. Informant.

Ingeniero, feminine ingeniera.

Noun.   Sir,   madam,   mister,   boss,
anthropologist, hello, hey, buddy, depending
of the contex.

Investigación

Noun. Research.

Jalar

Verb. Smoke marihuana, leaving a place,
depending of the context.

Jamear

Verb. To eat.

Jato

Noun. House, to sleep, depending of the
context.

Jefe

Noun. Sir, boss, depending of the context.

Ladilla

Noun or Adjective. Parasite, nasty person, depending of the context.

Maestro, feminine maestra

Noun. Sir, madam, buddy, friend, hey, depending of the context.

Malcriado, feminine malcriada

Adjective. Impolite.

Mancha

Noun. Group of friends, spot, depending of the context.

Manyar

Verb. Eat, see, watch, look, depending of the context.

Marco teórico

Noun. Model, theory, assumption, depending of the context.

Misio, feminine misia

Noun or adjective. Without money, poor, depending of the context.

Mosca

Noun or adjective. Fly insect, smart, sneaky,

Munanquichu

Verb. Quechua. Do you want?

Nancy

Adverb. Nothing.

Oe

Interjection. Hey!

Pachamama

Noun. Mother Earth.

Pacharaco, feminine pacharaca.

Adjective or Noun. Snob, stupid, inferior, depending of the context.

Paja

Noun or adjective. Beautiful, nice, pleasant, depending of the context.

Parientes

Noun. Relatives.

Pata

Noun. Friend, guy, man, person, depending of the context.

Pe

Adverb or conjuction. Well, then, depending of the context.

Pirañita

Noun or adjective. Thief.

Pituco, feminine pituca

Noun or adjective. Snob, rich person.

Plata

Noun. Money, silver, depending of the context.

Posada

Noun. Shelter.

Puriy

Verb, Command, Quechua. Walk

Rajar

Verb. Form a bad opinion and conclusion of somebody.

Rico, feminine rica.

Noun or adjective. Rich person, rich, good taste, yummy, depending of the context.

Ripuy

Verb, Command, Quechua. Go way.

Sacar la vuelta

Expression. Be sexually unfaithful.

Saco largo

Expression. Be dominated by the wife.

Sangrar

Verb. Losing blood, take advantage of somebody with money, depending of the context.

Sapo

Noun or adjective. Smart.

Sed

Noun. Need to drink something, thirsty.

Señito

Noun. Madam.

Serrucho, feminine serrucha

Noun. Person who is from the sierra (also serrano or serrana. In another context means traitor.

Terruco, feminine terruca

Noun and adjective. Terrorist

Tombo, feminine tomba

Noun. Police officer.

Trabajo de campo

Noun. Fieldwork.

Trago

Noun. A drink.

Wawa

Noun. Child.

Waykicha

Noun. Little brother.

You can add more words...

62

You realize that this list of words is incomplete of course, so you have to study very hard. Yes, most words are slang, but they are part of language anyway. In other words, I am trying to say that you need a Peruvian Spanish tutor before going to Peru. If you don't know slang, context, body language, hidden intentions, and local concepts, your fieldwork will be totally wrong. I think it is better to hire a Peruvian anthropologist, but this is not the case, right?

64

Source: César González Aguilar. Huanchaco,
Peru.

Peruvian worldview revolves around demons.

Money

All my anthropologist friends of from United States and

Europe told me the same thing: money is the most

important 'skill' to do a fieldwork! It is a shame that this is

the reality of anthropology now.

I think money is important in Peru, but it's not the most

important 'skill', in any case, you need money to give

presents and to buy food and drinks for your informants.

Generosity is always widely welcomed.

66

Source: César González Aguilar. Huanchaco, Peru.

Peruvians are hard workers.

Ethics

Cultural relativism, categories, concepts, theories, labels, names, ideas, terminology are crucial, but they are tricky.

All societies and communities are equals? All traditions deserve respect? Think twice! Cultural relativism is a tool, no more than that. We need universal values, universal decency, so, if we are confused with these ideas, if we don't know what it's wrong and what it's right, then we need to study harder the basic concepts.

68

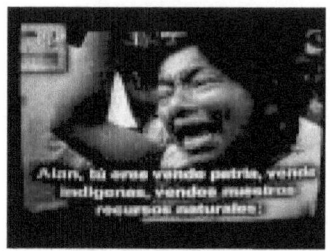

Source: César Blanco.

We can find online thousands of themes for our research in Peru. This very short video on YouTube shows a variety of Peruvian facts: racism, injustice, genocide, ethnocide, corruption, social conflicts, multiculturalism, colonialism, domination, migration, hates, anticulturalism, anomie, and so on.

Source: Carlos Quispe.

Juan Santos Atahuallpa, Plaza de Atalaya, Region de Ucayali. Peruvian heroes and their stories are numerous.

Source: Julio César Farfán

Knowledge, erudition, scholarship, information, libraries, and books are tools. Anthropology should be the practice to build a better world.

Gear

Bread

Peruvian anthropologist Carlos Quispe from Chinchero says that most anthropologists work in the Andes region where farmers have many dogs, therefore, he adds, you will need bread to feed them if you want to come back with your two legs!

Notebooks, Pencils, Camera

Write down and record important issues as soon as possible because our minds change everything. We need small notebooks, small pencils, and small cameras. Mini cameras now take very nice pictures and they record high quality videos. Try not to take notes in front of informants, and ask permission for taking pictures and publish them. Ideal anthropologists never take notes in the field because they really 'live in the culture.' You never take notes in situ about what you do at your fast food favorite place, right? If you want to inform others about your favorite place, just go home and write down what you know. If you really 'are' in the culture, then you can do the same thing.

Source: Jhonny Ramos. Huanchaco, Peru.

Visual anthropology means a great deal of variety of interpretations.

Source: Calalo Sánchez.

No computer, no fieldwork.

Theory

Yes, you need theories and methods, but when you are in the fieldwork, you capture the reality, and the reality becomes more important than theory. Theory is not a supreme commander. In fact, you are in the fieldwork to challenge all theories. After your fieldwork, all theories will be different. Remember this all the time while you are in the field. If you just do your fieldwork with theory, then your do nothing. All theories are incomplete or wrong, so remember this all the time!

Source: Sheila Arroyo. Universidad de San Antonio Abad del Cusco.

Fine Peruvian anthropologists: Dr. Jorge Flores Ochoa, Dr. Ricardo Valderrama, and Dr. Washington Rozas.

Source: Julio César Farfán
Peruvian anthropologists Carlos Quispe and Julio César Farfán (Pelucas.) There is a huge difference between an alien anthropologist and a local anthropologist.

Information

You need information to do your research, but be careful please, there is a lot of information in the fieldwork. You don't need everything, so focus on your theme, and remember always:

HOW YOU OBTAIN INFORMATION IS VITAL IN YOUR FIELDWORK.

If your information assures that some people are literate because they themselves state that fact to you, that information means nothing. You need to

prove it with other tools and techniques

because   people   say   too   many

incoherencies.

Source: Julio César Farfán

Peruvian anthropologists from University of San
Antonio Abad of Cusco.

Source: Julio César Farfán

Identity, education, literacy. Anthropologists can improve many lives.

Remember, fieldwork is not only the collection of raw data.

Source: Rocio Motta

Doctor Oscar Paredes Pando and his students doing fieldwork in the Amazonia.

Humanity

YOU ARE A HUMAN BEING AND YOUR INFORMANTS ARE HUMAN BEINGS TOO. YOU ARE NOT A PHYSICIST AND YOUR INFORMANTS ARE NOT MATERIALS. WHILE TRAINING AT SCHOOL, IF THEY TAUGHT YOU HOW TO BE AN ANTHROPOLOGIST AND A COLD OBSERVER WITHOUT INVOLVEMENT, THEN THEY WERE WRONG. WHEN ANTHROPOLOGISTS ARE INSINCERE, INFORMANTS ARE UNSURE WHETHER THEY ARE FRIENDS OR FOES. YOU ARE NOT GOING TO THE FIELD TO MAKE ENEMIES, YOU ARE GOING TO THE FIELD TO MAKE FRIENDS

INSTEAD. GOOD ANTHROPOLOGISTS EMPOWER INFORMANTS TO CONTROL THEIR LIVES. IN OTHER WORDS, WE ANTHROPOLOGISTS MUST HELP OUR INFORMANTS SOMEWAY.

Source: Ricardo L Sabogal

Peru is really a beautiful country.

Source: Rommel Gonzáles

Peruvian happiness and Peruvian poverty are two anthropological important facts.

Source: Carlos Quispe.

The inclusion of Peruvians in their own country
is another interesting theme.

Source: Julio César Farfán

Popular justice, exclusion, domination, colonialism, liberal economy, slavery, and so on.

Source: Julio César Farfán

Pictures, exoticism, and stories are not the most important goals. Welfare and justice are.

92

Source: Julio César Farfán

Do you want to help people or use them?

SOURCE: JULIO CÉSAR FARFÁN
FIELDWORK IS NOT ONLY DESCRIPTION. FIELDWORK IS TO IMPROVE QUALITY OF LIFE.

Source: Carlos Quispe

People's biographies reveal personal sentiments and social problems. We can help people if we know them.

Training

Good physical and mental conditions are essential for an anthropologist. You are going to walk a lot in Peru and you are going to deal with new and bizarre things everyday. You are not going to stay at the your comfortable desk reading books and playing with the computer. The best anthropologists are walking and having conversations almost all the time. I know a lot of them, they are not famous, they cannot publish books, they cannot afford nice schools, they must work hard to support their families, they do the real work in the field but their names are never on papers or on luxury books, and they are normally from poor countries like Peru. The best important part of any training is these values, rules, and principles:

HONESTY

RESPECT

SINCERITY

Theories? Concepts? Categories? Etcetera, and etcetera are nothing without these values.

Source: Julio César Farfán

Dignity, a strong sense of duty, and respect are crucial in the fieldwork. Main anthropologist's duty is to improve quality of life of victims of injustice.

Source: Carlos Quispe
Anthropologists can predict the
needs of future generations
because they work with people's
culture, therefore they
understand sentiments,
environment, organizations,
beliefs, habits, behavior, and
ways of life.

Source: Carlos Quispe.

Teaching and learning, learning and teaching. Anthropologist Carlos Quispe is teaching and learning in the field. Farmers are teaching and learning in the field too. Remember, we all are learners and teachers, and main anthropologist's concerns are people, culture, and justice..., and not corporations.

Source: Maquela Rozas

Female Peruvian anthropologists' skills and expertise are world famous.

Source: Carlos Quispe. Chinchero, Cusco.
Peruvian Anthropologist from Chinchero,
Cusco, says: 'don't forget to bring bread to feed
aggressive farmer's dogs!'

Relationships

Peruvian anthropologist Herman Pancorbo says that our relationship with the community and our informants are very important in our fieldwork success. Pancorbo believes that relations determine the quality of data and results. So you have to find the kind of person you could depend on, and on the

other hand, you have to be
sincere and honest, and
this is very difficult
because most anthropologists
hide information, and
because a lot of
anthropologists work for
abusive governments, abusive
armies, abusive mining
companies, abusive
corporations, abusive people,
and abusive NGOs.

anyway, remember, you are the strange person in the field. Your informants are in their home, and you are only visiting their homeland.

Source: César González Aguilar. Huanchaco, Peru.

Folks drinking Chicha, the Peruvian drink.

Source: Herman Pancorbo.

Education is of vital importance. The teachings of Anthropology have a profound effect on well-being at the present time because of multiculturalism and globalization.

Source: Enrique Tantaleán Calle

Friendship and amusement are two important values in Peruvian culture.

108

Source: Lorenzo Zelaya

Peruvian anthropologist doing fieldwork in Perugia, Italy. A Peruvian anthropologist can also study European aristocrats.

Source: Maquela Rozas

Peruvian female anthropologist from Cusco.

Source: David Mottoccanchi.

Local anthropologists, to the best of my knowledge, are the best fieldworkers because they are professional anthropologists and they have firsthand knowledge about their own culture.

Source: Carlos Quispe

The best anthropologist is the local anthropologist.

Many unwelcome alien anthropologists support exclusion because they deny local anthropologists.

SOURCE: MAYCOL LÓPEZ CEDRÓN.
NAIVENESS, HAPPINESS, AND CALMNESS ARE SOME PERUVIAN FEATURES.

SOURCE: LORENZO ZELAYA
PERUVIAN ANTHROPOLOGIST
DOING FIELDWORK IN PERUGIA,
ITALY. WRONG
ANTHROPOLOGISTS BELIEVE
THAT ONLY THE 'RICH'
NORTHERN ANTHROPOLOGISTS
CAN STUDY THE SOUTHERN
RURAL 'POOR'.

114

Source: Maga González, Huanchaco Beach.

Nicer people usually live in small towns.

Techniques

We need techniques of course: participant observation, interviews, surveys, all these tools for sure, but we have to perform them in a natural way. When anthropologists interview informants in an artificial atmosphere, something is wrong with the data, and imprecise data cause wrong information. If the anthropologist is a nice person or maybe a good friend, then fieldworks will be good ones. If informants trust us anthropologists, they consequently will give us good information.

The best way to learn something about a particular community is to really live in the community for at least one year. This is very difficult because many communities are uncomfortable. Many anthropologists live in nice places close to the communities, but that is a bad trick.

Source: Ricardo L. Sabogal.

Participant Observation 'is the strategy' in anthropology.

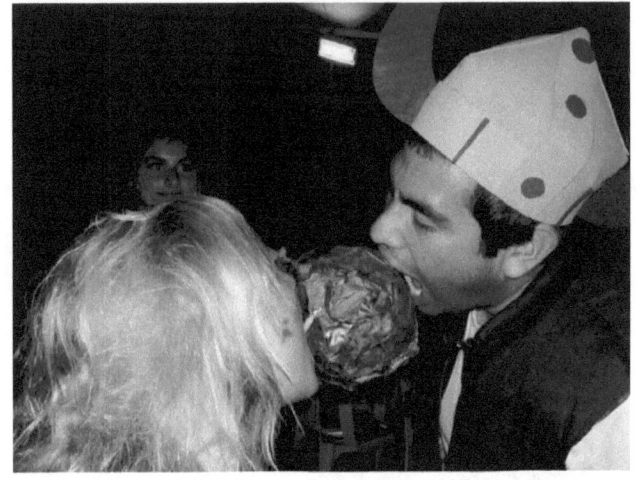

Source: Calalo Sánchez.

Participation is the anthropological technique.

SOURCE: MAGA GONZÁLEZ.

PERUVIAN TAMAL IS DELICIOUS AND UNIQUE.
YOU HAVE TO EAT EVERYTHING!

Source: Ricardo L. Sabogal.

Detailed observations uncover cultural phenomena.

Source: Edwin Rodríguez Valle.

Fieldwork is not a vacation. The hard, tough, honest anthropologist is always welcome. Peruvian anthropologist Edwin Rodríguez working in his own land.

Source: Julio César Farfán

Professors Aurelio Carmona and Jorge Flores Ochoa with Cusco University's students. If you go to Cusco, you must study these eminences' works.

Consequences

What are the consequences of doing our research? There will be bad consequences? Good consequences? We don't know? We must know the consequences! We want just to publish books? Just investments? Just knowledge? Money? Power? Privilege? Fame?

We ponder the consequences before our fieldwork and we take the consequences after our results.

Source: Jhonny Ramos. Huanchaco, Peru.

Carnaval and palo cilulo.

Questions?

You must develop proper questions, and the meanings of these questions must be the same for you and for your informants. Surveys, interviews, and observation guides must be well prepared to get accurate information.

In addition, you have to be a reliable person. If you lie once, the fieldwork is finished and you have to go home and find another place for your fieldwork.

THE BEST QUESTIONS ARE NOT DIRECT QUESTIONS; ON THE CONTRARY, THE BEST QUESTIONS ARE OBSERVATIONS, CONVERSATIONS, AND GENUINE INVOLVEMENT. YOU SHOULD OBTAIN INFORMATION THROUGH NATURAL CONVERSATIONS, BUT THESE CONVERSATIONS MUST HAVE GOALS TO OBTAIN THE RELEVANT INFORMATION, AND ALSO, OF COURSE, YOU SHOULD BRING SOME SMALL GIFTS FOR YOUR INFORMANTS. RECIPROCITY IS VERY IMPORTANT IN ALL CULTURES.

YOU SHOULD TAKE A FIELDWORK ASSISTANT TOO. IF YOU ARE A WOMAN, THEN YOU WILL NEED A

LOCAL MALE ANTHROPOLOGIST; IF YOU ARE A MAN, THEN YOU WILL NEED A LOCAL FEMALE ANTHROPOLOGIST.

COUPLES CAN HAVE ACCESS TO MORE PLACES AND SITUATIONS.

QUESTIONS ARE THE BASE OF OUR FIELDWORK, AND IF OUR QUESTIONS ARE WRONG, EVERYTHING IS WRONG. MOREOVER, QUESTIONS ARE NOT MERELY SENTENCES. WHAT DO YOU THINK ABOUT AUTHORITIES? THIS QUESTION ALONE IS NOT A QUESTION IN OUR FIELDWORK BECAUSE ALL QUESTIONS INCLUDE

CIRCUMSTANCES, MOOD, MANNERS, RELATIONSHIP, INTENTIONS, SUBLIMINAL MESSAGES, TIME, PARTICIPANTS, AND SO ON.

BETTER THAN A QUESTIONER OR CURIOUS ANTHROPOLOGIST IS A NATIONALIZED AND RESIDENT ANTHROPOLOGIST WHO LIVES IN THE LOCAL CULTURE.

Source: José Venegas. Huanchaco Beach.

Small towns, tranquil places, and relaxed people are the best combination for a good fieldwork.

Source: Joel Ucañán

Interviews and surveys are two anthropological tools.

Observation

I remember an anthropologist who was
staring at us in the Amazon jungle many
years ago. He also stared at local people in
amazement for exactly one hour. In the
meantime, good colleagues and I were
making some observations and inquiries of
our own. We learned later that this kind
of attitude is an issue that bothers people,
and we learned that we have to observe
naturally. Best observers are local people,

not foreigners, strangers, or outsiders.

That anthropologist who was staring at us

did not care anyway because he was a

mercenary who was looking for 'free'

merchandise as plants, minerals, artifacts,

or any precious thing. Do you want to

perform a better quality of observation?

Undoubtedly, you need a local

anthropologist.

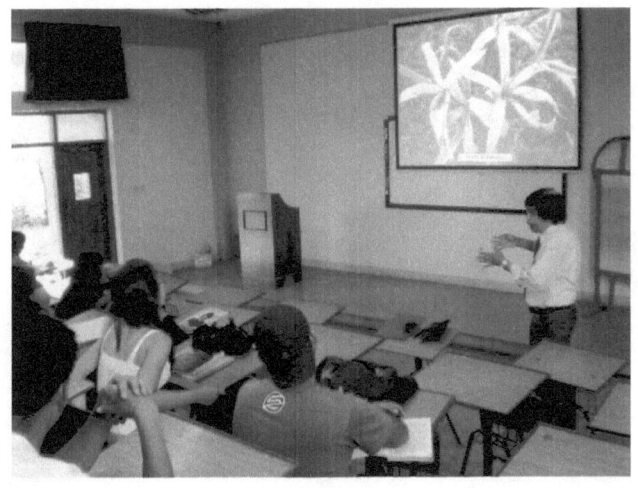

Source: Ricardo L Sabogal

Anthropologist José Becerra Castañeda from University of Trujillo, Peru. Discussion and critique aid anthropological advancements.

Source: Rocío Motta

Anthopologist Oscar Paredes Pando's students in the Amazonia. University of San Antonio Abad of Cusco's alumni are experts in Andean and Amazonian anthropology.

SOURCE: EDWIN RODRÍGUEZ VALLE.
PERUVIAN ANTHROPOLOGISTS WORK
EVERYWHERE ON THE EARTH.

136

Source: Angel Ramiro Romero Pacheco.

Production of ethnographic film, photography, and new media is not the final goal. These visual anthropology tasks are means to promote justice and better quality of life of innocent victims.

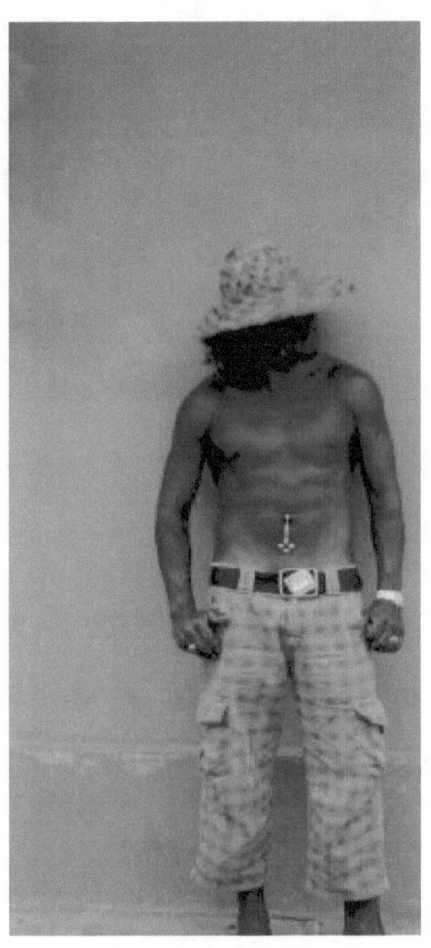

Source: Jhonny Ramos. Huanchaco, Peru.
Peruvian culture is unique and universal.

Source: Angel Ramiro Romero Pacheco.

Visual anthropology is becoming more and more popular thanks to new technology.

Unfortunately, Peruvian anthropologists lack of equipment in spite of their excellent skills.

Themes

Selecting a theme as being the best of many alternatives is not a nightmare. I believe, of course, personal preference to be a requisite for an enjoyable and suitable fieldwork, and for sure, everybody can find or discover themes everywhere. Just this simple instance, we listen in Peru to somebody saying offensively: "Ese es un cholo ignorante!" [That guy is an ignorant mestizo!]. No a word more, no a word less. We already know the meaning of the sentence in English, also, we know that the tone of the sentence means in Spanish and English something pejorative, insulting, and crude to every person. Fortunately, anthropology is amazing because we can discover dozens of themes in this sentence alone: Do you like gender? Do you like politics? History? Evolution? Conflict? Racism? Social network? Kinship? Religion? Folklore? Values? Traditions? You can link `*cholo*' with any of these preferences and you will find something unexpectedly for sure. You need just imagination, and imagination is vital in the fieldwork to discover new realities and new solutions.

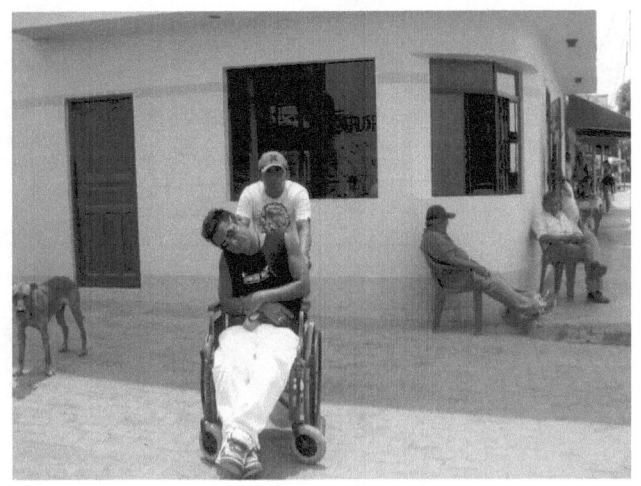

Source: Luis Alexander Urcia Arroyo. Huanchaco, Peru.

Ancient Peruvian fishermen.

Source: Carlos Antonio Ferrer. Huanchaco, Peru.

Buzo and his relative. Peru is full of astonishing and interesting characters.

Source: Rommel Gonzáles

Peruvian world champion Piccolo Clemente from Huanchaco, Peru. Surfing is art? Surfing is sport? Surfing is tradition? Surfing is lifestyle? Anthropology of surfing has a responsibility to research ancient Peruvian surfing.

Source: Rommel González

New houses in the capital of Peru. Centralism in Peru is a shame. Peruvians are subjected to all manner of indignities.

Source: Liga de Tabla Hawaiana de Trujillo, Huanchaco, Peru.

Main Peruvian values are work, education, progress, family, friendship, and honesty.

Experimentation

We can experiment in the fieldwork without harming people. Put a Ferrari next to a poor woman in pain and you will see real people's values.

Maquela Rozas, Peruvian anthropologist, suggests that we have to research before our research. This means we have to do a previous sample research. She thinks that if we research directly without prior study, then the informants will 'laugh at us'.

We can perform controllable experiments with the Internet giving hypothetical information to our network and analyzing the people's reaction to it.

Source: Ricardo L Sabogal. Huanchaco Beach.

World famous handicraft.

148

Sins

Most popular Anthropologist's sins are:

Promises

Too many anthropologists promise too many things. They promise help, support, money, letters, presents, and so on. They do that because they owe informants a debt of

thanks, therefore they want
to pay their dues to society.

POSEY ATTITUDE

Pretentious anthropologists
become fool and
untrustworthy to the eyes of
the informants. I remember an
anthropologist who had dinner
with people from Cusco, Peru.
He made lot of faces trying
to impress falsely the

farmers, and that was a very bad idea because people can feel bad and good vibes. No one wants moody people giving off bad vibes.

Make Money

Making money is not a sin, but making money in fraudulent ways is a different story. The problem is that anthropologists think

they are helping people when in
fact they are taking
advantage of them. Too many
anthropologists make unfair
use of people for one's own
benefit. There are too many
mercenaries today.

EGOCENTRISM

Many colleagues suffer of
egocentric intellectual
perception and they are the

center of the research. The
ideal motivation
of the anthropologist should
be the pursuit of cultural
justice: people living together
in peace and justice. The
worst motivations are
prestige, money, personal
recognition, and awards.

Hidden intentions

Unethical and hidden intentions such as 'stealing' knowledge to be used against the local population are more popular now than in the past. Armies, corruptive corporations, mining companies, pharmaceuticals, drug dealers, organized international body of criminals, collectors, and others are hiring bad archeologists and anthropologists to do the dirty job.

Greed

Wealth and power have always been valued, and many anthropologists do not escape from this very old tradition. Colonialism and imperialism in this 21st century is stronger than in the past. The mining companies, organizations, and enormous corporations continue to abuse with the help of some anthropologists and archeologists without morals. It is disgraceful that

many archeologists and
anthropologists continue to be
an important part of the
abusive domination.

Demand

Some researchers demand that

informants must give them

facts and stories, made as if

by right.

These anthropologists are

'entitled' to ask

authoritatively.

156

NOTES

Religion

Religion and politics are extremely important in the fieldwork and they are very similar in many aspects. People filled with single-minded zeal for religious or political causes are very much alike and they are present everywhere. Are you an atheist? Are you agnostic? Are you communist? Are you liberal? Are you religious? Each person has a set of beliefs, consequently, by definition, this is a kind of religion, and our beliefs affect our worldview and our relationship with our informants. Our beliefs will be present all the time in the fieldwork whether one likes it or not.

Source: Rommel Gonzáles. Huancavelica, Peru.
Peruvian Catholicism, domination, looter, ethnocide, genocide, holocaust. Anthropological aspects of injustice have not been sufficiently studied despite the widespread nature of this fact in the context of abuser-abused relations in Peru.

Mind

Your mind should be relaxed because anxiety and stress are bad elements in the fieldwork. Your Mind enables you to be aware of the world and your unique personal experiences, to feel, to think, and to have a particular opinion about someone or something. The point is, of course, that you don't make the entire world a focus of attention: you

must be precise. Yes, your mind is aware of the whole context, but it concentrates on your thesis only. Your questionnaires, your surveys, your guide to interviewing, and your guide to observation will help you to remember your particular interests.

Source: José Venegas. Huanchaco Beach.

Sand, sun, and culture are a good option.

Expectations

What are your expectations? Something will happen in the future after your fieldwork in Peru? Something better will happen to your professional life? Something better will happen to your personal life? Something better will happen to your country, to your university, and to your government? Something better will happen in Peru, in the community? Something better will happen to the informants? Informants surely expect the best outcome; authorities expect great things of anthropologists; and community residents where you work expect local and personal improvements. Human beings in general have high expectations for their future. Always remember this fact.

SOURCE: GIANCARLOS URCIA
PERU IS RUSTICITY AND SIMPLICITY.

Justice

Anthropologists work on many issues, but always related to humanity and culture.

However, anthropologists are not only scientists, they should promote also justice. Anthropologists have to have genuine respect for people, and the quality of being fair is very important. Culture means that we live peacefully together and therefore everything that pulls us apart is anticulture. Injustice is one anticultural element that is growing fast nowadays. We, anthropologists, must eliminate anticulture.

Justice promotes culture, peace, values, decency, and better quality of life. Injustice *promotes violence, anticulture, domination, poverty, and richness.*

SOURCE: ROMMEL GONZÁLES
PERUVIAN WORLD CHAMPION PICCOLO CLEMENTE FROM HUANCHACO.
ANCIENT PERUVIAN SURFING IS A VERY INTERESTING TOPIC.

Source: Carlos Antonio Ferrer.
Huanchaco, Peru.
The history of Peru is the history
of injustice.

Writing

We have to write every day about our research on paper. Normally, we write papers to somebody else, as at matter of fact. We usually present our papers to our superiors, and unfortunately, our superiors will shape our paper and our whole fieldwork.

You are a rebellious young dreamer, I know that, and for this reason can you tell me, for instance, what are you going to do when you indicate that the authorities are corrupt and your boss refuse to admit the necessity of providing such information?

Teaching

You have to teach always anthropology in order to let people know about our science, about culture, and about humanity. Society knows some ideas about physics, ecology, and astronomy, but our society knows almost nothing about anthropology and culture. Anthropology is fascinating, and we anthropologists have to teach anthropology to society. Professional anthropologists are determined to do their duty, and society should show more consideration for anthropologists because human culture, anthropologists' expertise, plays a crucial role in restoring human values in this materialistic world. Injustice is a cancer sweeping across countries and continents. Teachers, nurses, and police officers are underpaid, and in fact, housewives who are the main teachers and instructors, are unpaid and they don't have benefits.

Source: Luis Alexander Urcia Arroyo. Huanchaco, Peru.

Ancient Peruvian fishermen.

Working

There is a vast number of

Possibilities for

anthropologists: aid agencies,

advertising agencies, e-

businesses, mass media

companies, research centers,

international businesses,

schools, universities,

multinational corporations,

mining companies, non

governmental organizations,

nonprofit organizations,

governments, and surely any

organization needs

anthropologists. Today the

majority of jobs for

anthropologists are created in

the international private

sector and in the national

governments with

international responsibilities.

Multicultural education,

multicultural businesses,

multicultural relationships,

multicultural communication,

multicultural human resources,

multicultural organizations,

multicultural management,

multicultural costumer service,

multicultural economies,

multicultural Projects,

multicultural developments,

multicultural Products,

multicultural conflicts,

multicultural negotiations,

multicultural hospitals,

multicultural knowledge,

multicultural ideas,

multicultural inventions,

multicultural technologies, the

list is infinite.

The Promising future of anthroPology is around the corner.

Source: Liga de Tabla Hawaiana de Trujillo, Huanchaco, Peru.

Catholicism, processions, and saints.

Source: César González Aguilar.

Huanchaco Beach is a real paradise.

180

Source: César González Aguilar.

Peruvian honest people work against corruption and central domination.

Source: César González Aguilar. Huanchaco, Peru.

Caballitos de totora.

Source: Carlos Antonio Ferrer.
Huanchaco, Peru.
Old Huanchaco Beach.

Source: Solo Computo.

Peruvian ways of life are so many.

Source: César González Aguilar. Huanchaco, Peru.

Peruvian Piccolo Clemente is the champion of the world.

Source: Felipe Rodríguez Rivas. Claretiano
School, Trujillo, Peru.

Old pictures tell emotional dramas and
unique biographies.

Source: José Venegas. Huanchaco Beach.

Cultural landmarks are important: Old Don Pepe Restaurant was a point for surfers.

Source: Tito Lescano, Huanchaco Beach.

Small towns are full of character.

GRAPHICS

BOTH SIDES ARE PART OF OUR JOB, BUT THE

RIGHT SIDE IS FAR MORE IMPORTANT.

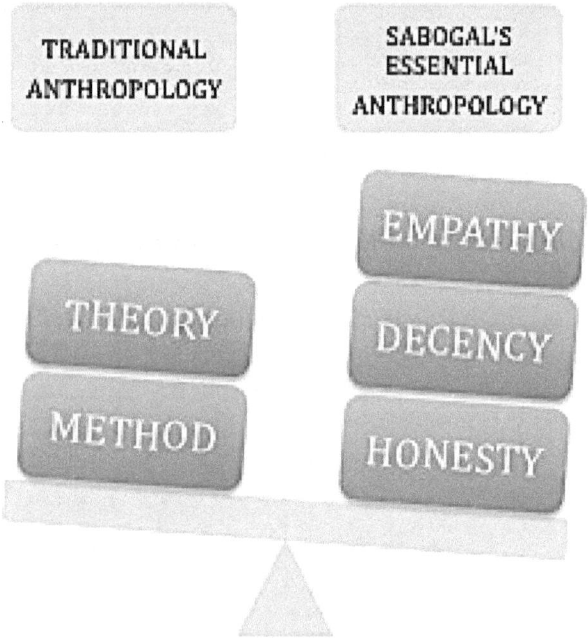
TRADITIONAL ANTHROPOLOGY
SABOGAL'S ESSENTIAL ANTHROPOLOGY
EMPATHY
THEORY
DECENCY
METHOD
HONESTY

Traditional anthropology faithfully follows classic theories and methods' plot. Essential anthropology does the same thing plus empathy, decency, and honesty. Although classic intention is also to encourage empathy, decency, and honesty, these values are not mandatory. In fact, many anthropologists and archeologists forget these basic principles. Essential anthropology affirms that theory and method without decency are useless because anthropology is a science that deals with human beings. We anthropologists will have to find a way of dealing with our feelings, and the best way is decency.

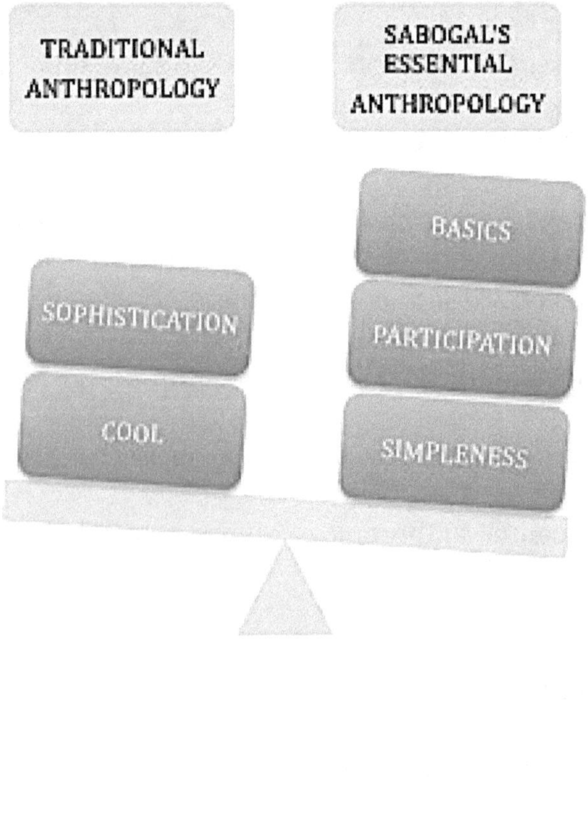
TRADITIONAL ANTHROPOLOGY
SABOGAL'S ESSENTIAL ANTHROPOLOGY
BASICS
SOPHISTICATION
PARTICIPATION
COOL
SIMPLENESS

Traditional anthropology uses sophisticated jargon. Essential anthropology uses this professional jargon plus plain and simple language. Traditional anthropological language maintains broken links between society and anthropologists; sophistication maintains useless and oligarchical academicism. Sophistication plus basics and simpleness allow theoretical analysis and social participation as well. Sophistication tends to be forgetful, therefore we must remember the basics: we are all human beings living one universal culture with diverse manifestations and aspects. Culture is the way we live together.

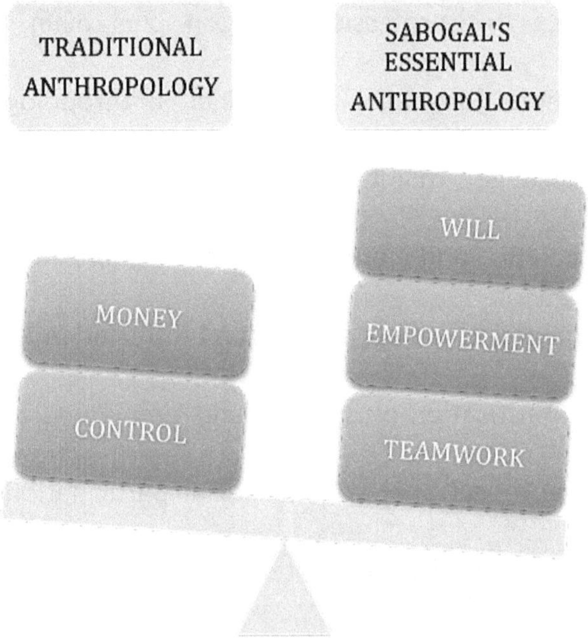
TRADITIONAL ANTHROPOLOGY
SABOGAL'S ESSENTIAL ANTHROPOLOGY
WILL
MONEY
EMPOWERMENT
CONTROL
TEAMWORK

Traditional anthropology needs money because is very luxurious, and results and image are very important. The whole anthropological operation is under the control of a team of experts. Essential anthropology needs money too, but if there is no money, then there will be anthropology anyway. Some anonymous Peruvian anthropologists are fine examples of this fact. Essential anthropology employs teamwork because utilizes the combined action of anthropologists and informants. Also, essential anthropology empower people and enable them to control their information.

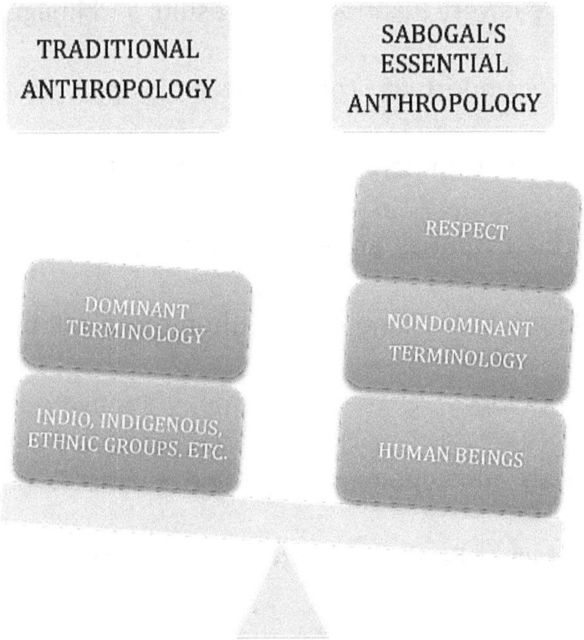
TRADITIONAL ANTHROPOLOGY
SABOGAL'S ESSENTIAL ANTHROPOLOGY
RESPECT
DOMINANT TERMINOLOGY
NONDOMINANT TERMINOLOGY
INDIO, INDIGENOUS, ETHNIC GROUPS. ETC.
HUMAN BEINGS

Traditional anthropology needs specialized terminology to analyze sociocutural phenomena. The problem is that this terminology causes discrimination and domination. Ethnic group is always 'poor people', indigenous is always 'poor people', primitive people are always 'poor people'. If people from a rich community belong to these categories by definition, amazingly, they have nice names. On the contrary, essential anthropology respects human beings.

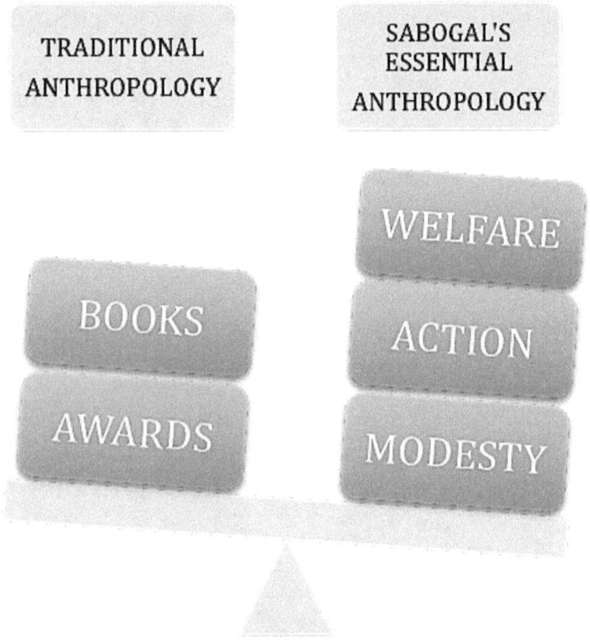
TRADITIONAL ANTHROPOLOGY
SABOGAL'S ESSENTIAL ANTHROPOLOGY
WELFARE
BOOKS
ACTION
AWARDS
MODESTY

Traditional anthropology loves books and awards. Of course, this is normal because anthropologists deserve recognition for their work. Essential anthropology loves them too, but welfare of informants and action to reach this goal are more important.

Books and awards don't mean egocentrism or selfishness. Rather, they mean modesty and hard work.

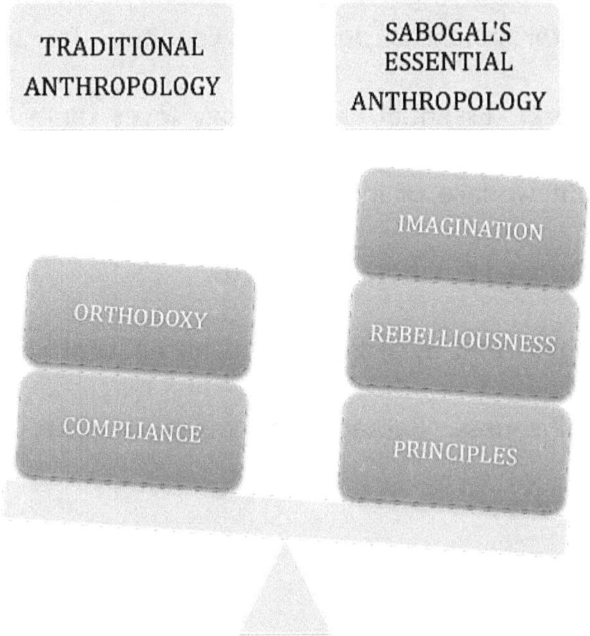
TRADITIONAL ANTHROPOLOGY
SABOGAL'S ESSENTIAL ANTHROPOLOGY
IMAGINATION
ORTHODOXY
REBELLIOUSNESS
COMPLIANCE
PRINCIPLES

The appalling compliance with anthropological orthodoxy shown by traditional anthropology is a clear signal about the direction of decline.

Essential anthropology skills are imagination, rebelliousness, and principles, and indeed morally correct behavior and attitudes are more important than abstract orthodoxy. Besides, imagination and rebelliousness are necessary to improve theories and methods.

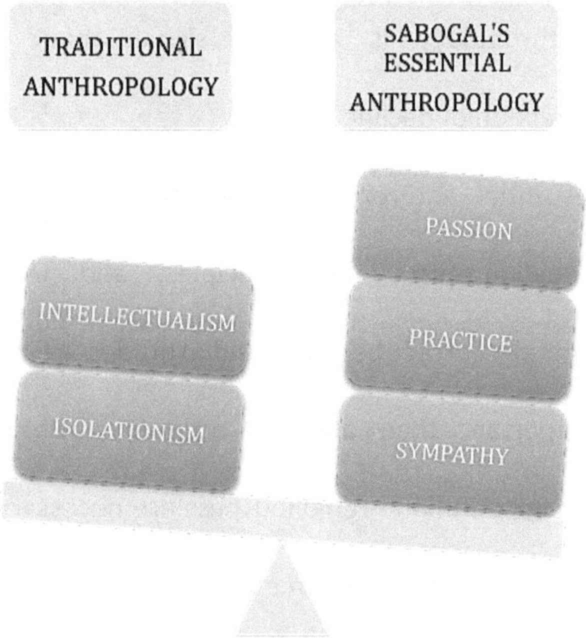
TRADITIONAL ANTHROPOLOGY
SABOGAL'S ESSENTIAL ANTHROPOLOGY
PASSION
INTELLECTUALISM
PRACTICE
ISOLATIONISM
SYMPATHY

Traditional anthropology loves intellectualism, but this position on anthropology and this attitude toward the society generate isolationism.

Essential anthropology prefers passion, practice, and sympathy to pure intellectualism: passion for justice and quality of life for all; practice of humanity and generosity; and sympathy for the victims.

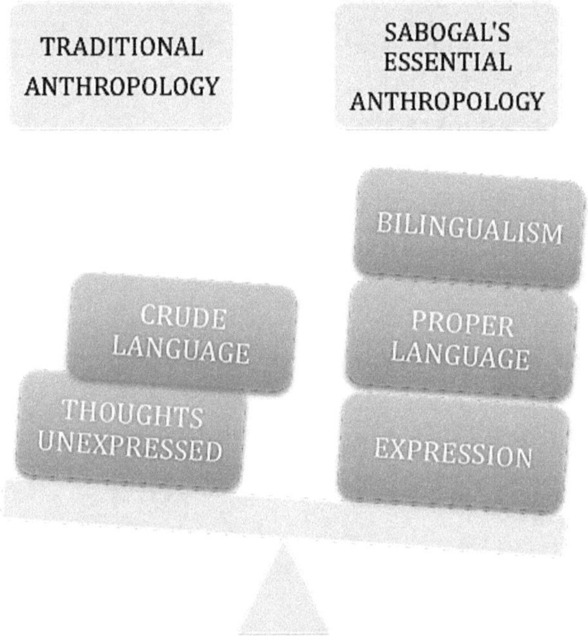
TRADITIONAL ANTHROPOLOGY
SABOGAL'S ESSENTIAL ANTHROPOLOGY
BILINGUALISM
CRUDE LANGUAGE
PROPER LANGUAGE
THOUGHTS UNEXPRESSED
EXPRESSION

Traditional anthropology is very busy and very productive. Traditional anthropologists have not time to learn genuine Spanish, Quechua or other languages. Local information is less important than orthodox theory and orthodox method.

Essential anthropology is bilingual because informants and their information and needs are more important than orthodox theory and orthodox method. Essential anthropology avoids cold anthropology and cold language. The best anthropologist is an expressive partner.

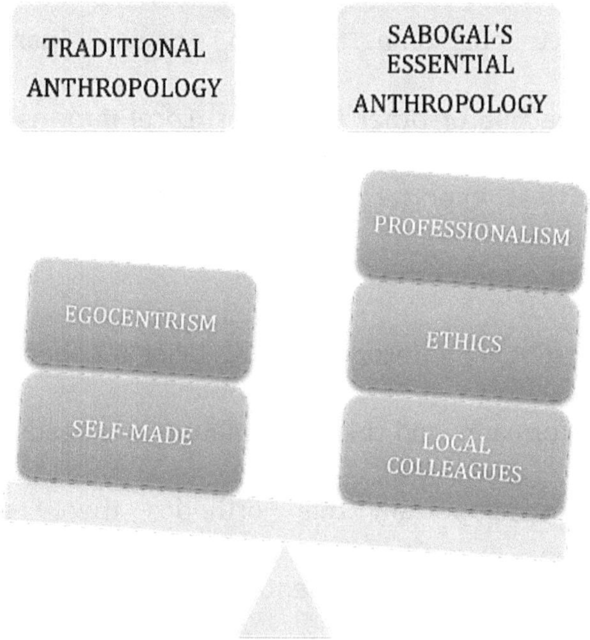
TRADITIONAL ANTHROPOLOGY
SABOGAL'S ESSENTIAL ANTHROPOLOGY
EGOCENTRISM
SELF-MADE
PROFESSIONALISM
ETHICS
LOCAL COLLEAGUES

Traditional anthropology defends egocentrism and self-made anthropologists, but we know that self-made people don't exist and we know that egocentrism is the antithesis of anthropology because anthropology is a social science. Too many alien anthropologists and archeologists ask for help from local colleagues and informants in a furtive way. These researchers capture information from local anthropologists and archeologists but they don't recognize these naïve experts.

Essential anthropology recognizes contrarily everybody's job.

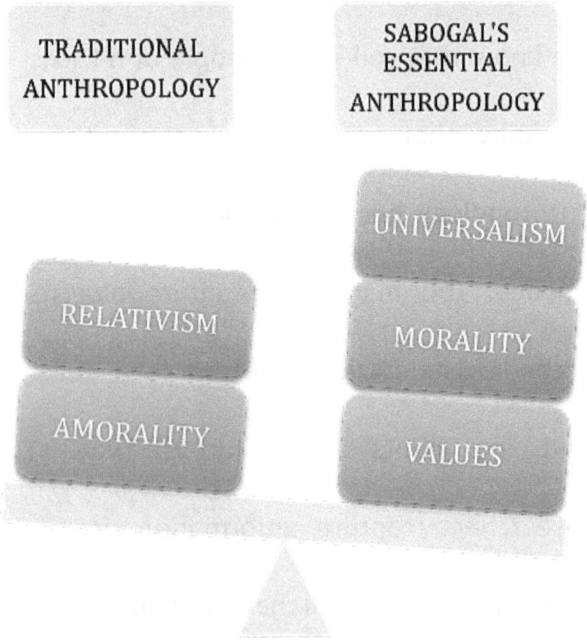
TRADITIONAL ANTHROPOLOGY
SABOGAL'S ESSENTIAL ANTHROPOLOGY
UNIVERSALISM
RELATIVISM
MORALITY
AMORALITY
VALUES

Traditional anthropology adopted relativism and amorality long time ago because of the cultural diversity. Besides, relativism tries to avoid judgments and try to promote equality. This position is consistent with its intellectualism.

Essential anthropology has morality and values because real professionals respect universal rules and values and because essential anthropology's goal is a genuine culture of universal justice.

TRADITIONAL ANTHROPOLOGY

SABOGAL'S ESSENTIAL ANTHROPOLOGY

COMMUNICATION

TECHNICAL QUESTIONS

DEVOTION

THEORETICAL PREJUDICE

LIVING IN

Traditional anthropology's concerns are theories and categories for detailed analysis of data. Also, traditional anthropologists have preconceived opinions that are no based on experience. They don't live in Peru, they are only visiting, and their language and questions in the field are too technical, consequently, there is no clear communication between these anthropologists and informants.

Essential anthropology prefers direct communication and a long time stay in the community, and indeed devotion and enthusiasm are important to accomplish this.

TRADITIONAL

ANTHROPOLOGY PROCESS

LEARNING
- CLASSIC THEORIES AND CLASSIC METHODS

THEORIES/ METHODS
- EUROPEAN AND US ANTHROPOLOGISTS ONLY

ANTHROPOLOGISTS
- THEY DEFEND IDEAS THAT MAY SUPPORT BOTH SUPREMACY AND VICTIMS AS WELL

IDEAS THAT MAY SUPPORT SUPREMACY /VICTIMS
- MATERIALISM
- COGNITIVISM
- CROSS-CULTURALISM
- PERSONALITISM
- DIFUSSIONISM
- ECOLOGISM
- FEMINISM
- FUNCTIONALISM
- HISTORICISM
- POSTMODERNISM
- EVOLUTIONISM
- STRUCTURALISM
- SYMBOLISM

ESSENTIAL

ANTHROPOLOGY PROCESS

LEARNING
- CLASSIC THEORIES AND METHODS
- PLUS PERUVIAN THEORIES AND METHODS

THEORIES/METHODS
- EUROPEAN, US ANTHROPOLOGISTS, PLUS ANTHROPOLOGISTS FROM PERUVIAN SCHOOLS: TRUJILLO, CUSCO, PUNO, AYACUCHO, IQUITOS.

ANTHROPOLOGISTS
- THEY DEFEND IDEAS THAT MAY SUPPORT SUPREMACY AND VICTIMS AS WELL

IDEAS THAT MAY SUPPORT SUPREMACY/VICTIMS
- MATERIALISM
- COGNITIVISM
- CROSS-CULTURALISM
- PERSONALITISM
- DIFUSSIONISM
- ECOLOGISM
- FEMINISM
- FUNCTIONALISM
- HISTORICISM
- POSTMODERNISM
- EVOLUTIONISM
- STRUCTURALISM
- SYMBOLISM
- ANDINISM
- INCASISM
- MOCHISM
- INSURRECTIONISM

Why may theories support supremacy or victims? You will find out many cases by yourself for sure.

I can give you here only some examples:

Evolutionism, materialism, and ecologism: Some societies are better than other societies, as a result of this conception their civilized citizens are entitled to dominate other uncivilized people.

Structuralism and functionalism: Domination, injustice, abuse, and so on, have their part and role in any society.

All theories have two sides, and don't worry, you will find both sides in all theories.

Thank you for reading this manual and God

bless you.

218

INDEX

D

E

224

NOTES

PAINTING BY RICARDO L SABOGAL